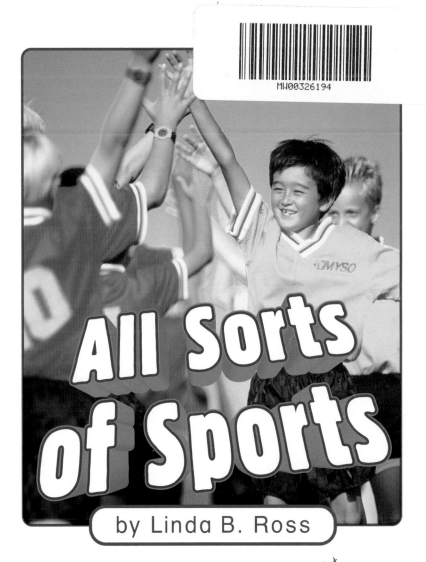

All Sorts of Sports

by Linda B. Ross

Harcourt

Orlando   Boston   Dallas   Chicago   San Diego

Visit *The Learning Site!*

www.harcourtschool.com

You can try all sorts
of sports. Lots of kids
play sports. What a
good time they have!

She saw the ball and kicked it. Now she'll score for her team.

It's a good morning to be out! What a good day for this sport!

4

Is this the sport for you
to try? Mr. Short thinks so.

This sport is fun. It is called T-ball. You hit the ball and run.

Look at him go! He could be thinking, "I'll score for our team!"

You need a ball for this sport, too. You have to run back and forth so you can shoot the ball.

Is this the right sport for you?
Do you like to kick? If you do,
this sport is for you!

He goes down the hill!
You need a sled for this sport.
Don't forget your hat, too!

He wants to go one more time. So he has to climb the hill.

When you try a new sport,
jump in and go for it!